THEY
TRUSTED
IN
GOD

THEY TRUSTED IN GOD

ERNEST BRADY

Rev. date: 08/11/2020

To order additional copies of this book, contact:
Xlibris
UK TFN: 0800 0148620 (Toll Free inside the UK)
UK Local: 02036 956328 (+44 20 3695 6328 from outside the UK)
www.Xlibrispublishing.co.uk
Orders@Xlibrispublishing.co.uk
811706

CONTENTS

PROLOGUE

The purpose of this book is to encourage the reading, understanding and application of the Word of God. As a baptised believer in the Lord Jesus Christ I am convinced that this is the chosen means by which an almighty and Holy God has revealed His desire to establish a personal relationship with His created beings who have been separated by sin.

A characteristic of those who have such a personal relationship is that they

Trust in God

Do not be afraid, Moses heard the words,
the bush before him alight
I need you to rescue my people from Egypt,
see, I am aware of their plight
and my presence will be with you as
you stand before the Pharaoh
Following miraculous signs and wonders
my people he will let go.

Do not be afraid Joshua heard the words;
facing the city of Jericho
As I was with Moses, I will be with you,
so this is what you must do.
Obeying the Lord, and following His plan,
the walls of the city fell down
Joshua went on to subdue the land,
his victories knew no bounds

Do not be afraid, Gideon heard the words,
hiding within the wine press
'A man of valour', you will defeat the
Midianites, who my people oppress.
As Gideon obeyed the Lord's directions
a miraculous victory took place
300men with trumpets and torches were
used to demonstrate God's grace.

Do not be afraid, Mary heard the words,
in a small town in Galilee
You shall be with child and shall give
birth to a son, the Holy One is he
a virgin she trusted her Lord, "may it be
so", her response to these words
and so in the fullness of time, the Son
of God entered the world.

Do not be afraid, the twelve heard the
words, many times over three years
in incidents beyond their control, Jesus
gave strength to quell their fear
As they witnessed the miraculous it became
clear He was no ordinary man
He was the Messiah, none other than
the Son of God and man.

Do not be afraid, we too hear these words, in our world today,
when faced with trials and troubles as
we seek to follow His way.
Through the Word of God the Spirit seeks to encourage us all,
revealing Jesus as the living Lord, the Saviour of us all.
God

ABRAHAM

A tale of two hills

An old man climbed a mountain

a task he must perform,

his heart was broken, but his faith was sure.

On mount Moriah.

The God he trusted, he was prepared to obey

for so long He had shown him the one true way

and promised and delivered so much.

On mount Moriah.

His son was with him, pleased to be there,

a sacrifice was needed, but he knew not from where.

he asked the question ; "the Lord will
provide" his father replied

On mount Moriah.

The story unfolded, the man's hand was stayed

a ram was revealed;on the altar it was laid

and the son's life was spared.

On mount Moriah.

The years have passed, another sacrifice takes place

a Father's Son is offered freely

but His hand is not stayed

On Calvary.

The "lamb" is the Son,

God, the Father, gave him up, since

He loved the world so much.

On Calvary.

What Abraham was spared

Our heavenly Father has endured,

the perfect One was slain, the world by love was saved.

On Calvary.

Then let us bend the knee and worship

the one who died and rose again.

The Law's demand was met; "it is finished" was His cry

On Calvary.

AMOS

a man with a message

Amos, was just a man from Tekoa

A herdsman and a dresser of trees

He came to Bethel from Judah

With a message that did not please

He warned of an end to their life of ease

The impending judgement of a holy God.

He never claimed to be a seer

A prophet or even a prophet's son

But his message began "thus says the Lord"

And he spoke the words of the Holy One

A warning of troubles that could not be averted

For they had tried God's patience and broken his Law

They had ill treated the weak and exploited the poor

Thus their fate was determined by the deeds they had done

For this they would suffer; the Lord's will must be done

His words would come true in the fulness of time

The Assyrians came and the northern kingdom fell

A salutary warning to ourselves, in the 21st century, as well.

BARNABAS

The Encourager

The story of Barnabus is rarely told, but
its impact however is plain.

We first hear of him in Jerusalem as he
gives money to the common purse,

by selling land he owns and giving all the
proceeds to be used in the Lord's name.

Significantly. As he relates this, Luke states that
his name means 'son of encouragement'.

Barnabus, remained a faithful and
trusted member in Jerusalem.

So when following the martyrdom of Stephen, news of
the scattered believers gaining converts in Antioch

reached them, he was selected to investigate what was
happening and report to the apostles in Jerusalem,

After assessing the situation, he fetched
Paul from Tarsus and together they spend a
profitable year teaching the believers.

Their ministry is clearly effective and results in the
believers being the first to be called Christians

An indication of Paul's stated intent, as he later wrote 'to
know nothing amongst you but Christ and Him crucified'.

On hearing from a prophet called Agabus of a
potential famine in Judea they send him and Paul to
Jerusalem with a gift for their fellow Christians.

Having successfully completed this task they returned to
Antioch taking with them a young man called John Mark.

Whilst in prayer the fellowship there are led by
the Spirit to set Paul and Barnabus apart,

They are charged with the mission to spread the
good news of the gospel of Jesus Christ.

With the blessing of the church therefore, and taking
Mark with them as an assistant, they depart.

Sailing from Selucia, they start their journey
in Cyprus, the birthplace of Barnabus.

Having success in their ministry as the move
across the island, they lead the procoul to faith
following a demonstration of the power of God

, For reasons not recorded by Luke, Mark returns
to Jerusalem An event which later caused
friction between Paul and Barnabus.

When they move on to Antioch in Pamphylia they are invited
when visiting the synagogue to speak from the Word of God.

Using his understanding of the scriptures Paul
demonstrates that Jesus is the Christ, the risen Lord.

In response he is requested to return the following Sabbath
when many are brought to faith in Christ, including gentiles

The knowledge of the gospel begins to spread throughout
the region, but not all respond to it favourably.

As had been the case since the outset there were
those who opposed the message, especially strict
Jews who objected to the inclusion of gentiles.

Consequently they were forced to move on to Iconium
where their ministry continued to flourish.

However the antagonism is again stirred up
and for safety they travel on to Lystra

Here, a cripple is healed in the name of Jesus, and this is
mistakenly attributed to the appearance of greek gods.

As spokesman, Paul is deemed to be Hermes,
Barnabus to be Zeus, and they are 'worshipped'
as such by the people of Lystra.

Their refuusal to accept these accolades causes
the mood to quickly change and Paul finds himself
being stoned and left for dead outside the city.

The believers however gather and pray; Paul
revives, returns to the city, moves on to Derbe then
retraces his steps encouraging the believers.
Returning by a different route and preaching
and teaching as they travel Paul and Barnabus
arrive back in their home church Antioch.
As commissioned to do, a report of how the
Lord has blessed them on their journey is
delivered to the fellowship of believers.
Thankful to the Lord for His grace and mercy on
their travels Paul and Barnabus remain in Antioch
for some time enjoying the fellowship.

The final historical reference to Barnabus in
scripture highlights his personal ministry of
encouragement, but results in his leaving Paul.
In planning a return to see how the young churches
are faring, Paul considers it unwise to take
Mark who had previously deserted them.
Barnabus, seeing the potential of the young man,
disagrees and as a result he separates from Paul.
Interestingly he is subsequently proved right in
his assessment since Paul, when a prisoner in
Rome, describes Mark as 'a faithful friend'.

CAIN AND ABEL

Right and Wrong

Go forth and multiply, God had
instructed them before the Fall,

and this is what they did, though now
their issue was tainted by sin.

Their offspring were never to experience
the blessings of Eden,

but they knew that unto the Lord for mercy they must call.

The need for them to seek forgiveness from the Lord

had doubtless been explained and
passed on by Adam to his sons.

A heartfelt sacrifice, being the means
for this function to be fulfilled

Cain, the farmer and Abel, the shepherd
thus offered their gilts to the Lord,

Cain brought some of the produce, he had grown, we read.

This then being offered, it would appear,
with little personal cost or thought.

Whilst his brother carefully selected from
amongst his flock a firstling lamb

For him, a costly sacrifice showing his love for God it seems.

The offering made by Abel found favour with God,
that of his brother did not His favour gain

Even so, we read of God counselling Cain,
warning of the imminent danger he was in

Relying instead upon his feelings, Cain gives
vent to his anger and kills his brother

Once again In love he is offered the opportunity
to repent but this also is in vain.

This story stands as a salutary warning to us
all, we are to 'do right and be accepted'

As we are reminded by James sin...'when
fully grown...produces death'.

Therefore let us, by the power of God's Spirit
within us, seek not to succumb to sin.

In so doing, we may 'do right'. and. by the
grace of God. in Christ be accepted.

CLEOPAS

Encounter in Emmaus

We had thought he was Messiah, Cleopas a shared their tale

The stranger who had joined them
seemed unaware of the detail

Jerusalem in tumult, a crucifixion
preceding the Passover Feast

Now friends were saying that the one who
was killed had risen from the dead!

The stranger listened attentively, then
began to express his views

Displaying a remarkably sensitive knowledge
of the history of the Jews

Explaining the scriptures to them he
enthralled them with his words.

Their journey now completed, he was
persuaded to stay and share some food.

The stranger took the bread, said a
blessing, then shared it with them

Their eyes opened to the truths they felt as
he had walked and talked with them,

This was their Lord, alive, as he had
promised – and then he was gone!

What they had seen was enough, they returned
to the city, convinced He was the One.

Thereafter their lives were changed, as
they joined with those who believed

Becoming part of the fledgling Church which
grew as the good news was received

Repent and believe, the message was spread;
the crucified One had risen that day

Salvation is offered to all who respond; the Holy
Spirit given to guide them on the Way.

DANIEL

God is faithful

Daniel prayed thrice to the One true God

Although the law decreed that he should stop

A practice he had established whilst in Babylon

he had determined that this would continue to go on

This law had been enacted because of the jealous thoughts

of those who disliked the role he held within the king's court

A foreigner who had succeeded due to his prophesey

They feared he would put their roles into jeopardy

Having flattered and persuaded the king of the day

a law was passed, that none could gainsay,

Whoever prays, breaks the law, the king had said,

They show a lack of respect and deserve to be dead.

To the lions lair Daniel was taken to die in great pain

The king had been tricked, but his remorse was in vain

So he prayed that Daniel's God might even then intervene.

He went early to the den, and was amazed at what was seen!

God protected his faithful witness
although he was securely bound

The lions mouths remaining closed, not
a mark on him could be found

A miracle had happened, king Darius was overwhelmed.

A new decree issued: Daniel's God was to
be worshipped throughout his realm.

ESTHER

The story of Esther in the Scriptures is unique

At no point In the narrative is God's name invoked,

but it is the theme of Providence that
makes the story complete,

It is set during the exile, in the court of an all powerful king.

The story opens with a description of the king's
power and the opulence of his court.

His word must be obeyed by all; the
queen Vashti being no exemption

When she does not respond to his
command to appear in court,

his furious reaction results in her being
stripped of her regal status.

We now learn of the beautiful niece of Mordecai a Jew,

Her parents having died when she was
young, he had brought her up.

Noted for her outstanding beauty the king was
unaware that she was one of the Jews.

Her name was Esther and she was eventually
selected to replace Vashti as queen.

Again in the Providence of God her uncle
overheard a plot to kill the king,

whilst he was keeping watch over his charge
sitting at the gate of the palace.

Through queen Esther the plot discovered
by Mrdecai was conveyed to the king

Having been verified by an investigation, the
event was written into the court records.

We are now introduced to an arrogant
nobleman who is favoured by the king.

Haman is elevated to high office and
revels in the way he is revered

The people bow in his presence but when
Mordecai refuses to do so it is reported and
he is given leave for revenge by the king

Haman:s fury extends to the nation also when he
learns Mordecai is a Jew, he plots to wipe them out.

He persuades the king that the Jews
threaten the stability of his kingdom,

and a date is therefore set for their annihilation
in all the land to take place

An edict being proclaimed to this effect
throughout the Prsian kingdom

Mordecai displays his sorrow at the news by
tearing his clothing and weeping in contrition

Refusing to be consoled by his niece he
pleads with her to petition the king

Reminding her of her heritage and intimating that
she may have become queen for a reason

An agreement is reached for a time of prayer and
fasting as Esther considers approaching the king

Again we recognise the Providence of God
in the king having sleepless night

He reads of Mordecai saving his life, and asks Haman
how he should honour a deserving subject of the king

the advice of Haman who thinks he is to
be the recipient of this honour

results in Mordecai being rewarded for
having saved the life of the king.

Humbly, Haman therefore has to escort Mordecai as
he rides the king's horse wearing the king's robe!

Esther puts herself in view of the king and is asked to
approach; he notes something is disturbing her

She informs him that she will tell him when he
attends a banquet she is going to have for him.

Esther also asks the king to invite his
friend Haman to join her.

Unknown to the court, Haman has decided to hang
Mordecai, the cause of his perceived humiliation

However he attends Esther's feast.as the day
draws near for the annihilation of the Jews

On the second day, the king offers to grant
a request for anything to his queen

Esther then pleads for her life and that of her
people revealing herself as one of the Jews

On learning that Haman has instigated this
plan the king orders his execution.

Haman who had arranged for a 75 foot scaffold to be
built to hang Mordecait then died on it in his place.

The law to kill the Jews could not be repealed but
a further decree gave them the right to resist

Thus in the Providence of God Mordecai's words
came true; Esther was in the right place.

God's name never appears in the text, but
His influence pervades the entire tale.

ELIJAH

Contest on Carmel

Fire shall be the proof, but fire not made by man.

In response to prayer, must this deed be done,

As a sign of power, to be seen by everyone.

Ba'al or Yahweh would be the victorious one.

The scene was set upon Mount Carmel,

As the prophets of Ba'al began their ritual.

A sacrifice was chosen and laid upon the altar,

They began to call out and they did not falter.

In desperation they cut themselves and cried,

But response from their 'god' was never supplied.

Perhaps he's away or asleep; the taunting came,

until exhausted, they ceased; all their efforts were in vain.

The lone prophet of Yahweh, Elijah, also was there,

God's altar was rebuilt and the offering prepared.

"Pour water on it" he instructed, "make sure it is soaked.

Our God will respond when his name is invoked".

"Let it be known you are God...."; then the people saw

The fire fall from heaven as they gazed on with awe

The offering was taken and God's answer was clear,

Elijah's prayer was answered; the One True God was there!

The contest now was over; Ba'al had been proved to be

against the God of Israel, an impotent adversary.

For God alone in the heavens reigns

So we must place our trust in His holy name.

Many years have now gone by, but this fact is true:

There is only One True God and He still loves you.

no longer by fire does God speak to us today

but now through his Son; sent to show us the Way.

Jesus lived and died, then rose again for you.

"He who knows me" He said "knows my Father too".

He brings forgiveness and freedom from sin

To all who believe and put their trust in Him.

GIDEON

'Marvellous in our eyes'

When Gideon threshed his corn he did so in a winepress,

hiding from the Midianites, who were
intent the Isrealites to oppress.

His family was considered to be one
of the smallest of the clans,

as the youngest of his father's sons,
he was an insignificant man.

Imagine his surprise when he was addressed

as a warrior, to whom God would give great success!

In a series of incidents he showed his integrity,

And is known as a Judge in the annals of history

His greatest task was to defeat the Midianites.

It began with a large army responding to his call,

some 25,000, all armed and ready to fight.

But God said send away all those who are filled with fright!

The number now down to 10,000 brave souls

Go down to the river and drink, they were told

Only 300 lapped the water from cupped hands

These I will use to honour my name,
came the Lord's command!

The contest was strange, using trumpets and torches.

With a shout of triumph, and a blast on the trumpets

the torches were exposed, creating confusion in the enemy.

The battle was brief, the Israelites had the victory!

In no way could Gideon or his army claim to have won

Without the hand of God in all that was done

"'This is the Lord's doing and marvellous in our eyes'"

Is the only response to be made to such deeds, we must cry.

JOSEPH

The Dreamer

The story of Joseph is one of Providence and grace

Explaining as it does the reason why the exodus took place

He is the eleventh of the twelve sons of
Jacob, now to be known as Israel.

Joseph. The first born of Rachel, he was favoured
by his father creating discord in the family.

A situation exacerbated by his dreams which
he naively shared with all his family

Each of these concerned imagery which
clearly indicated Joseph's superiority,

not only over his brothers but also in one,
concerning the cosmos over his whole family!

The hatred of his brothers eventually
led to their intending to kill him

However providentially, his life was spared
as passing slave traders bought him,

His father being duped into believing his
life had been taken by wild beasts,

Joseph now found himself sold on to be
a servant in an Egyptian home

Here the Lord was with him. Blessing him
and also his master Potiphar's home,

Potiphar, who was captain of the royal guard, accordingly
promoted him to be in charge of the household.

Sometime later Joseph became the object
of her attraction for his master's wife.

Having rejected her advances, she falsely accused him
and Potiphar had him jailed for attacking his wife

God's hand however continued to be with
him during his sojourn in prison.

As a result of his integrity he was soon acting
as the jailors assistant whilst in prison

Fellow prisoners a baker and a cupbearer shared
dreams which God enabled Joseph to interpret.

They had both incurred the wrath of their
employer the Pharaoh himself,

Incarcerated whilst the Pharaoh deliberated
on what should be their fate,

The cupbearer's dream indicated that release would
come in a few days followed by restoration

In contrast the baker would in a few days time be
released to face execution rather than restoration.

When this happened Joseph asked for his unjust
treatment to be made known to Pharaoh

Two years however were to pass before disturbing
dreams were had by the Pharaoh.

The need for these to be explained triggered the cupbearer's
memory and Joseph was brought from the prison,

Under the guidance of the Lord Pharaoh's
dreams are explained by Joseph,

he tells Pharaoh that God is warning him, of a severe famine
would be preceded by years of plenty says Joseph,

His suggestion that during the good years surplus
grain might be stored is welcomed by the Pharaoh,

And in recognition of this Joseph is freed to organise
things, given a role answerable only to the Pharaoh.

In the providence of God Joseph, as indicated by his
childhood dreams, becomes one who exercises power.

Egypt therefore survives during the years of
famine which also affects Joseph's family,

Egypt sells it's surplus, and along with others, his
brothers arrive to buy grain for their family.

Not recognising their brother in his elevated role as an
Egyptian official they are however known by Joseph.

After ascertaining his father is alive, Joseph reveals
his identity to his brothers and is reconciled,
Eventually in the providence of God, Israel moves his
family to Egypt settling in Goshen where they prosper.

JOSEPH (N.T)

My Unique Role

"The news from my betrothed Mary, when
it came, filled me with dismay,

I was a respected carpenter in the village,
I could not afford a scandal.

I believed her to be a God fearing and
honest young virgin maid,

but now she was telling me that she was
to be with child;..miraculously!

In order to avoid the inevitable disgrace
that this would produce,

I was determined to break off our engagement privately,

but a message from the Lord, in a dream
confirmed her words as truth,

and so began the wonderful tale of the
birth of the Lord Jesus Christ.

Mary then became my wife, but she remained
pure until the birth of her promised son.

As such whilst with child, she visited
her elderly, cousin Elizabeth,

amazingly, she too, in her old age, had conceived
and was soon to deliver her son John.

She acknowledged the special nature of Mary's child
and in response Mary thanked and praised her Lord.

Being of the lineage of David, I went to the town of
Bethlehem, the call for a census having been made.

Thus it was that prophecy was fulfilled and the
incarnation took place whilst we were there,

the angels announced this to the shepherds,
who were led to worship the babe.

Following the birth in the poorest of circumstances
I found us a home in which to wean the child.

Some twelve to eighteen months later,
Mary and I received a surprise visit.

Arriving at our home in Bethlehem was a caravan
bringing a group of Magi with an extraordinary tale!

They had travelled for many miles and addressed
Mary's son as a king; worthy of their worship!

presenting him with symbolic gifts of
gold, frankincense and myrrh

They reported how a sign had indicated to
them the birth of a king in Israel

which had led them to make the journey; Informed
by Herod of a prophecy regarding Bethlehem,

they had been led by the presence of a star to
acknowledge him as the promised king of Israel.

Warned by the Lord not to return to Herod who meant to harm the child they returned home by a different route.

On not hearing from the Magi, Herod was still determined to remove his perceived rival.

Basing his decision on the time when the Magi thought the birth had taken place he ordered the death of boys up to two years old.

Once again I received a message via a dream to flee from Bethlehem before the soldiers arrival.

As a family then we stayed in Egypt until learning of Herod's demise we returned to Nazareth."

The final reference to Joseph by name, is when as a diligent parent he takes the family to Jerusalem.

It is recorded that Jesus was twelve years old causing consternation by remaining in the city.

Having been found as he declared 'about His father's business' we read that Jesus returns with them as an obedient son.

As an adult, Jesus is referred to as the carpenter's son but Joseph is not mentioned by name again;...his role having been fulfilled.

MAGI

Gifts fit for a King

We hear the story every year, as part of the Nativity tale.

How strangers from a foreign land began
a journey that led to Israel

Guided we are told, by a new star they had spotted in the

heavens;

a sign they believed, of a new king having
been born somewhere on the earth.

Scripture is clear on how much importance
they attached to their quest.

On arrival, they headed for the palace
expecting to be welcomed as guests

by bringing their greetings for the new king;
instead they filled Herod with dread

Aware of prophecies about messiah, he
ascertained when this event took place

He then sent his visitors to Bethlehem, a small
Judaean town, and they travelled there alone.

Herod's advisers having explained where the
prophesied messiah would be born.

Feigning an interest, Herod suggested
they return with news of the child

whilst planning the demise of one he
viewed as a rival for the throne.

With joy they continued travelling, noting
the star was still to be seen in the sky

On arrival they were led to where Joseph,
Mary and their young son resided

Almost two years after the start of their trip,
they saw the One whom they sought

On bended knee they worshipped Him,
revealing the gifts they had brought.

Gifts 'fit for a King' were then presented; also
symbolic of the life he was to live.

Gold speaks of a Kingly presence
despite the humble life He lived.

The gift of frankincense speaks of His priestly
role; offering one sacrifice for sin.

Finally the myrrh which indicates how
this was to be achieved by Him

The ministry of Jesus is thus represented
by the precious gifts offered to Him

For the King of glory came to offer
Himself as a sacrifice for our sin

To all then who in repentance and
faith place their trust in Him

there is offered eternal life through Christ
by the grace of a loving God

NAAMAN

Trust brings healing

Naaman was a rich man famed for his
bravery and military prowess.

Although respected by the King of Aram,
he suffered; from leprosy.

Among his servants, a Hebrew maid told of the
ministry of Elisha the prophet in Israel

On hearing this the King of Aram sent him to the
King of Israel, with gifts, saying 'make him well'!

This request was considered to be a ruse to cause war,
the King was In anguish and tore his robes as well.

Elisha then sent word ; 'send him to me, I will
show him there is a prophet in Israel.'

When he came, Naaman too was given a message
from Elisha's servant concerning his cure

This was seen as disrespectful by the proud commander
who expected at least to meet his deliverer.

He was further annoyed by Elisha's instructions
to him concerning what he should do

Go, bathe in the River Jordan seven times, he
was told, your skin will then be as new.

Finally, persuaded by his attendants who appealed to
his prowess, Naaman succumbed and did it…….

……after he bathed seven times the cure was
effective! Naaman was again whole and fit !

In joy he returned to thank Elisha, offering him
all the goods he had brought as well

These were refused by the prophet, who
attributed the cure to the God of Israel

Having unsuccessfully urged him to take the
gifts, Naaman recognised the God of Elisha.

He requested some of Israel's soil to
stand on as he worshipped ;

so Naaman returned to Aram, a cleansed and changed man.

The subsequent actions of Elisha's servant
provides a salutary warning to all mankind.

Seeking to make some personal gain, he lied to
Naaman, claiming Elisha had changed his mind.

But our God is not mocked, Elisha perceived Gehazi's
sin, warning him of the consequences of his action.

There being no repentance the punishment was grave, his
body became leprous to remind him of what he had done.

NEHEMIAH

Restoration

Their apostasy had resulted in the exile of the nation.

Having been settled in Babylon for several generations,

they were now permitted by the Lord to return to Jerusalem.

However the city remained in a state of ruin,

Nehemiah, a Jew born in exile, was a high
official in the court of the king.

When news of the state of the city reached
him, he was greatly distressed,

and following a prolonged period of prayer
this was noted even by the king.

Boldly, trusting in the Lord, Nehemiah explained
the reason for his being distressed.

As a result, he was not only given
permission to travel to the city,

but also the authority and the provision of
all the materials needed for its repair.

This situation does not honour the Lord he announced,
determined to restore the walls of the city

Moved to tears by how dishonouring to the Lord
he found things to be,when he got there

With the authority of the King and the materials
he had brought with him, Nehemiah began the
task of restoration by rebuilding the walls

Despite the opposition hey encountered, Nehemiah
encouraged the people by reminding them to trust in the Lord

Even though it needed them to build with a trowel
in one hand and a sword in the other,within a matter
of fifty two days they had rebuilt the walls !

The city had begun to be restored although far from
being as it had formerly been in all its glory.

Then in the presence of all the people Ezra the
scribe read the book of the Law once delivered
to Moses for their guidance by the Lord

As they listened, the assembly was moved to
tears of repentance, realising how far they had
strayed from the faith of their forefathers.

Crying out for His mercy they sought to reinstate
the sacrifices and practices described in the Law
dedicating themselves anew to their Lord

The city now being secure there was great
rejoicing as they praised God.

NOAH

The flood

The instructions given to Noah were explicit
giving details of all that would happen.

The Lord revealed the reason for His action
and the means whereby it would happen

All this would have been strange since it
had never rained upon the earth

Nevertheless with remarkable faith Noah
comp!every obeyed the Lord

His family too showed moral fortitude as they
gathered materials and the means for the work,

following Noah's directions as they were given
to him by the Lord, they built the ark.

no doubt this was accompanied by ridicule
and scorn during these years

from those who had no regard for the God whom Noah serves

In His forbearance the Lord caused two of
each creature to join them in the ark

and He instructed Noah to take more of certain
creatures with him as they entered the ark.

Then when the time was right, we
read, "the Lord shut them in"

The floodgates were opened, the rain fell, and all
on the earth perished because of their sin.

The rain continued for forty days but the sojourn in the
ark lasted for more than a yearComing to rest on mount
Ararat, Noah sought to discover the state of the earth.

Utilising two birds, a raven, (a scavenger) and a dove

Noah decided that life had returned to earth; as
an olive leaf was brought back by the dove.

On leaving the ark, Noah's first act was to
acknowledge the Lord in thankfulness.

with the building of an altar and the offering of a sacrifice.

The result is described as being a sweet
smelling savour to the Lord,

and there follows what we are informed are
the musings of God Himself, the Lord.

These are later shared with Noah and his sons;
God acknowledges the evil nature of mankind,

whilst being prepared to establish a covenant
promising never again to destroy mankind.

The rainbow, we are told, serves as a reminder
of this covenant to both God and ourselves.

Thus enabling the descendants of Noah and
his family to 'go forth and multiply'

PAUL

Paul in Philippi

Come over and help us, the man in the vision said,

So they left Troas and sailed to Macedonia not knowing why,

Paul and Silas having believed the vision to be Spirit led.

Having landed, they travelled to a cosmopolitan
city of both Jew and Gentile called Philippi..

On the Sabbath, they made contact with
a group who prayed by the river,

amongst them was a prominent Greek
business woman called Lydia.

On listening to the message of the gospel her heart
was opened by the Lord as they spoke to her.

After demonstrating her faith in baptism, she offered
hospitality to them and whilst there they resided with her.

During their stay they regularly preached
the Word by the river and prayed.

For several days a slave girl who made money for
her owners by telling fortunes pestered them.

Eventually Paul released her from the evil spirit that
possessed her and her powers were stayed.

Seeing their income curtailed the owners stirred up
resentment against Paul and Silas and a mob seized them

Dragged before the magistrates Paul and Silas
were beaten and thrown into prison untried.

Incarcerated and shackled, their trust in the
lord never wavered, at midnight they were
praying and singing God's praise!

As they sang the prisoners listened until a violent earthquake
caused shackles to fall and doors to open wide.

Fearing his charges had escaped the jailer came
trembling ready to kill himself in disgrace.

Paul's cry that all had remained and were safe provoked
the utterance "what must I do to be saved?"

Having been told to believe in Jesus and
then being instructed in what this involved
he became a believer in the Lord

Taking them into his home he tended their
wounds and fed and watered them.

Having done so he and members of his family were filled with
joy, being baptised after confessing their faith in the Lord.

The next day orders came for their release but Paul having
indicated that he was a Roman citizen refused to leave.

Fearing the wrath of the Romans, the magistrates
themselves came to apologise in person
and escorted them from the prison.

Returning to Lydia's home, Paul and Silas encouraged
the new believers before taking their leave

The young church established in Philippi grew
and prospered and in writing to them later
Paul speaks fondly of all they had done.

PETER

Pentecost

Jesus had left them to go to his Father.

How could they do what His love now demands?

They stay in the city the doors locked and barred,

to wait for His promise and obey His command.

They wait and they pray, not knowing the outcome.

The building was shaken, a wind blew amongst them,

Then tongues of fire touched them; their hopes were restored

with boldness they went forth, praising their Lord!

The people were baffled

as they heard in their own tongue: !

"The Messiah is Jesus, he has risen from the dead,

of this we are witnesses", were the words that they said.

Some mocked their behaviour, but Peter spoke out.

The prophet foretold this, it's proof of the truth

that Jesus, the Messiah; who on the cross our sin did take

has now risen and lives having died for our sake.

Repent, be baptised, he said, salvation is free

to all who respond in faith; listen to me!

At Pentecost then, the 'church' was born

as numbers were added and this message goes on.

RUTH

Providence

The story of Ruth is one that speaks of love and loyalty.

Her choice to stay with Naomi, affecting
the course of Israel's history.

"Your people shall be my people, and
your God mine", she said.

Ruth arrives in Bethlehem and gleans
barley so that they may be fed.

In the Providence of God, the owner is a
relative of the husband of Naomi.

Admiring her fidelity and evident beauty,
Boaz learns who this new girl is.

Throughout the barley harvest he
ensures her success in his field,

instructing his foreman to even deliberately
see that she lifts grain from their yield

In accordance with the rules of the Law at that time, a 'kinsman redeemer' had rights.

He could buy Naomi's land, but must also accept responsibility for her and Ruths' plight;

meaning he would be obliged to take Ruth as wife ensuring the family name lived on.

The nearest kin demurred, but Boaz was pleased to accept, and Ruth became his wife.

The Providence of God continues to be seen as Israel's history unfolds,

In the fulness of time Ruth gave birth to a son, Obed is his name we are told.

Little is known about him except that his son was Jesse, the father of David.

Destined to be the forebear of the Messiah, the son of God and Man.

SAUL OF TARSUS

A journey to Faith

The road was dusty and dry, as Saul
travelled with one thing in mind;

to stop these blasphemous lies and
punish all those he could find.

He had witnessed it first in the City; how
could they believe this........and die?

The man had claimed to be God, the
King and promised Messiah,

The High Priest had judged him; he
was clearly an heretical liar.

for such an offence he deserved to die and
nobody survived being crucified.

The light which had shone at noon was brighter than the day

their progress was stopped, they could
not continue on their way.

Saul was alarmed as a voice spoke his name:
"Saul, Saul why do you persecute me?"

The voice came from heaven and he fell down in fear

with awe he replied "Who are you Lord?"
and anxiously waited to hear.

The Lord spoke and told him that he had been
chosen; he would later know what he must do.

Three days of blindness and fasting as
he waited, and no doubt prayed.

A disciple, Ananias came, his Lord's will
to perform by giving him aid.

"Brother Saul, receive your sight" he
prayed - the persecutor was reborn!

Baptised and revived, the change was plainly on view,

in fellowship with those he once loathed, in
grace and understanding he now grew.

He became known as Paul and a relationship began
with Jesus that would control the rest of his life,

and so began on that day, the journey
of service to God on high.

A life summed up in the words he wrote
to the Christians at Philippi:

"FOR TO ME TO LIVE IS CHRIST

STEPHEN

The First Martyr

He was chosen to assist the apostles in Jerusalem,

with others who demonstrated their Spirit led wisdom.

With joy he sought to meet the needs of the poor,

he displayed his faith as he served Jesus his Lord,

for as he shared out the food he also shared God's word.

His ministrations to their needs gained for him the approval

of all who saw that he served them with love and grace.

But others were jealous of him and they lied bare faced,

stirring up a mob, just as had happened to Jesus before.

By the Sanhedrin he stood accused -
he had broken God's law.

Even they then were struck by his assurance and grace,

as the look of an angel seemed to spread over his face.

Moved by the Spirit he outlined God's dealings with man,

from Abraham, Jacob, and Joseph to the rescue by Moses

he showed that from the beginning
God was fulfilling His plan.

He continued with the history of the people of Israel

which often incurred the condemnation of the prophets.

Reminding them of Isaiah's dire warnings of judgement

proclaiming that their attitude had not yet changed.

For the death of the Messiah they were to be blamed!

This statement caused an immediate reaction of fury,

He was dragged away with the intention to stone him.

As the stones rained down on his body he looked up to see

The Lord Jesus standing, as if to say 'come and join me'

This vision enabled him to pray 'Lord please forgive them'

We may not be called upon to give up our life in this way,

But the call for us to uphold the truth remains to this day.

God's love requires that we are to care for the poor,

To obey His commands and place our trust in the Lord.

That we, like Stephen, receive our eternal reward.

THE WITNESSES CONTINUE…..

A task unfinished

Go into the world and make disciples of all.
With the Spirit's power this task was enacted,
the Ethiopian was baptised in response to this cal, I
and Cornelius, the first gentile, to the Church was added.

The apostle Paul then took up the reins;
travelling the Roman Empire proclaiming Christ crucified.
Preaching and writing, as he took great pains
to encourage the growing Church to commit their lives.

The ensuing centuries saw a continuing
spread of the Church,
sadly including division and acrimony
between those who would lead.
However at all times there were those who
trusted in God and were true to His Word,
guided by the Spirit, they expressed their
faith in both word and deed,

By the nineteenth century in Britain,
a new impetus was needed
William Carey expressed a concern to
take the gospel to lands overseas.
As a result he dedicated his life to serve the Lord in India,
becoming known henceforth as 'the
father of modern missionaries'

The twentieth century expanded the
range of missionary endeavour
including the translation of the Scripture
into the tongues of unknown tribes.
Five young Americanns gave their lives to
reach the Auca tribe in Ecuador,
and as a result thousands more trusted
in God and dedicated their lives.

Missionary tasks remain to be done, in our world today,
both in the wealthy West and in the so called Third world.
The continued need for the gospel to be
preached has changed in no way,
but how shall they hear if they are never told of God's Word ?

So we too must be prepared to trust in God,
being witnesses to the truths of His Word.
For it is by our words backed up by
action that the Church will grow
and hasten as it does so, the glorious coming of the Lord
as the victorious King of creation when
every knee to Him shall bow.

APPENDIX

Biblical refs

Abraham	Genesis	ch 22 vvs 1 -14
Amos	Amos	ch's 1-9
Barnabas	Acts	ch 4 vvs 6&37 ;
		ch 11 vvs 20-30;
		ch's 12 v 25 - ch 14 v 28.
Cain and Abel	Genesis	ch 4 vvs 1-14.
Cleopas	Luke	ch 24 vvs 13 - 35
Daniel	Daniel	ch 6 vvs 3 - 27
Elijah	1 Kings	ch 18 vvs 19 - 39
Esther	Esther	ch's 1 - 10
Gideon	Judges	ch 6 v 11 - ch 7 v 23
Joseph	Genesis	ch's 37 v 3 - ch 47 v 1
Joseph NT	Luke	ch 1 v 26 - 2 v21, vvs 39 - 52 &
	Mattew	ch 2 vvs 1 - 23.
Magi	Matthew	ch vvs 1 - 23
Nehemiah	Nehemiah	ch's 1 - 13
Noah	Genesis	ch's 6 v 9 - ch 8 v22
Paul and Silas	Acts	ch 16 vvs 19 - 40
Peter	Acts	ch 2 vvs 1 - 41
Ruth	Ruth	ch's 1 - 4
Saul of Tarsus	Acts	ch 9 vvvs 1 - 22
Stephen	Acts	ch 6 v 8 - 8 v 2

The Witnesses continue...

Printed in Great Britain
by Amazon

41826310R00037